STAY CONNECTED

Providing children with simplified mindfulness tools to live a connected life, while empowering them to stay true to themselves and giving parents an opportunity to connect with their children on a deeper level.

Written by Salpi Dunlap

Illustrated by Logan, London, and Lincoln Dunlap

Stay Connected
Copyright Text © 2020 Salpi Dunlap
Copyright Illustrations © 2020 Logan, London,
and Lincoln Dunlap
Edited by Michael Molenda

Second Edition printed in 2022

All rights reserved. No part of this publication may be reproduced or transmitted in any form or by any means, mechanical or electronic, including photocopying, recording, or otherwise, or stored in a retrieval system, without prior permission from the publisher.

For more information, contact:
Salpi Dunlap
salpi@staytruebooks.com
www.staytruebooks.com

ISBN 978-0-578-72383-9

DEDICATION

This book is dedicated to my kids. Thank you for believing in me and helping me become the person I am today.

Also by Salpi Dunlap:

Stay True

Stay Grateful

FOREWORD

"We all want to know that we are seen and heard." —Oprah

When I first set out to write this book over a year ago, I had a completely different idea in mind—even though the book was going to be based around the idea of staying connected. But during the pandemic of 2020, "staying connected" took on a whole new meaning.

Before the pandemic, part of this book was going to be about connecting in person—how important physical proximity is in the digital age. Boy, did that section go out the window, because in 2020, we all became the "Zoom-er Generation." So, I recast this book about finding a balance between connecting with humans and connecting with the Internet. We need to stay connected to ourselves, to our kids, and to our families, friends, and partners. Physical connection will always be an important human necessity. I'm so grateful I have my kids to hug.

I feel that *Stay Connected* works best if you and your child read one to two pages a day. Then, have a conversation, and ask each other the questions posed in each section. In just a few days, you'll notice a new connection forming in your relationship—a connection that comes from *communication*. Open communication is a cornerstone in healthy relationships. As a parent, you are building a solid foundation within your child that he or she will carry into adulthood. You may also notice changes in your relationships with others.

Now, more than ever, we need each other. It's very difficult for most people to live without social interaction. My daughter has had a particularly hard time not being able to see her grandparents and cousins during these socially distant times. She has been our family's champion of staying connected, as she is always the one planning events to spend time together as a family. Connection is essential for our overall well-being. Let's reclaim connection now.

Love connects us all.

CONNECT WITH YOUR BREATH

"If you want to conquer the anxiety of life, live in the moment. Live in the breath." – Amit Ray

I was really stressed out during the first few months of the pandemic. I was always reminding myself to stop and breathe whenever I was feeling scared or upset. I realized breathing helped me stay calm.

Each of the three books in the Stay True series starts with a breathing exercise. So, take a moment right now to focus on your breathing. Close your eyes and imagine you are at the beach listening to the waves. Take a deep breath through your nose as you count to five. Hold your breath for three seconds and breathe out through your mouth as you count to five again. Repeat these steps four times. As you're breathing, think about relaxing all the muscles in your body—starting from the top of your head all the way down to your toes.

Now, pay attention to how you feel after this breathing exercise. Are you more relaxed? Do you feel like you could focus a little more now than a few minutes ago? A breathing exercise is a great technique to use whenever you are feeling anxious or uncomfortable.

CONNECT WITH YOURSELF

"Stay connected with yourself and your truth. Nothing else really matters." — Khusbu Jain

Staying connected means making a conscious effort to notice and engage. It's important to keep in touch with our entire selves—our hearts, our minds, and our bodies. Sometimes, the best way to do this is to sit in silence. Observe your thoughts. Explore them. See how they make you feel.

What *are* you feeling? You could be experiencing a number of emotions. How does your body feel when you're happy? How does it feel when you're sad or angry? When you stop and pay attention to how your body is feeling, you are being aware and honoring your needs.

Do you ever spend time alone? I like to put music on and dance when no one is looking. Some other ideas for spending time alone are reading, playing outside, or using your imagination to create a new game. Make time for yourself every day and do something that makes you feel good. Make it a time free of screens—no phones, computers, televisions, or video games.

You should also practice speaking up for yourself. My son Logan got a haircut recently, and he didn't like how the barber cut his hair. But he didn't tell the barber how he felt. We used this situation as a learning experience. I told Logan that when you get a haircut and you don't like it—say something. Politely. Speaking up for yourself shows that you care about yourself, and that you are taking care of your needs.

CONNECT WITH YOUR HEART

"Your heart knows the way. Run in that direction." — Rumi

Every once in a while, check in with your heart. Ask what it wants and listen to it.

Make time for your *little* loves that warm your heart and fill you with joy. Is it painting? Drinking hot chocolate? Making sandcastles? Cuddling with your favorite stuffed animal?

Some of my kids' favorite things are playing soccer, baking goodies, making lemonade from scratch while listening to music, taking the dog for a walk around the neighborhood, and playing video games. Some of my favorite things are making puzzles, working on different book ideas, and listening to music. Make your own list of all the little things you enjoy doing, and see if you can do one of those things each day to make yourself smile. It's important to do something that makes you feel good every day.

CONNECT WITH YOUR MIND

"Chance favors the connected mind." – Steven Johnson

Did you know that sometimes we have a "monkey mind?" The monkey mind goes through a list of to-do items. It lists fears, both real and imaginary. It recalls hurtful things that happened in the past. It rehearses "what-if" scenarios over and over. Whew!

Quieting your monkey mind helps you find clarity, focus on the present, improve the quality of your sleep, increase calm, and make you happier. Here are some activities you can try:

MAKE THE MONKEY MIND YOUR FRIEND
Have a conversation with your monkey mind, and ask it, "Why are you so upset? What can I do to help you?" Most of the time, your monkey mind simply wants to be heard. But make sure you tell it that YOU are in charge! You can control the thoughts in your brain if you just try.

JOURNAL
Write down the things the monkey mind is saying. Once you get something out of your head and onto a piece of paper, your monkey mind will quiet down. Try it.

MEDITATE
Sit in a quiet place and focus on your breath for one to two minutes. (Remember those breathing exercises?) Meditation can help calm the monkey mind.

DISTRACT IT
Quickly notice three things surrounding you in the exact moment the monkey mind is tormenting you. Shift your focus away from what the monkey mind may be saying.

BELIEVE
Don't repeat the monkey mind's mantra of: "I can't do this—it's too hard!" Instead say, "I can do this if I keep trying."

Tree Pose	Child's Pose
	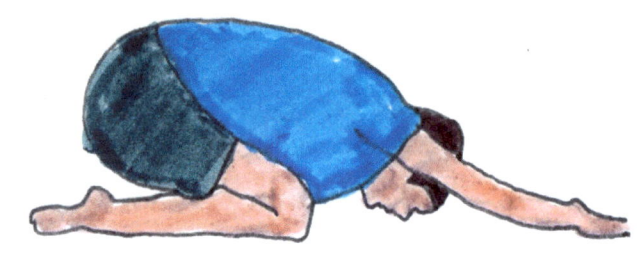
Warrior Pose	Downward Facing Dog

CONNECT WITH YOUR BODY

"To keep the body in good health is a duty. Otherwise, we shall not be able to keep our mind strong and clear." – Buddha

Take care of your body so it takes care of you—especially as you get older. Sleep well, eat healthy, do yoga, meditate, and exercise a little bit every day. I know these sound like a lot, but when we make them a priority, they always get done.

DO YOGA
Yoga teaches us to slow down, stay in the present, and treat our bodies gently. The child's pose, tree pose, and warrior pose are particularly good for grounding.

EAT HEALTHY
Eating healthy food keeps your body healthy. It's okay to eat junk food once in a while, but you need to eat healthy food every day.

DRINK WATER
Drinking lots of water each day keeps your body healthy, too. Did you know that 60 percent of our body is made up of water? Our bodies need water to stay hydrated and flush out toxins.

BOUNCE BACK
What do you do immediately after you get hurt? When my kids get hurt, I remind them to breathe through the pain and send loving thoughts to the part of their body that is hurting.

CONNECT WITH FRIENDS AND FAMILY

"Each friend represents a world in us—a world possibly not born until they arrive—and it is only by this meeting that a new world is born." – Anais Nin

Even during the worst times of the pandemic, we could connect by reaching out. It just takes a little creativity and effort. For example, you can always make time to call your grandparents or cousins who live in another town. Or send them a letter. Or try video calls.

You must also show interest in conversations with others. Engage with your senses, listen with your ears, and make eye contact. Find opportunities for meaningful conversations—which only happen when you are open and honest. A good way to remember this is to **THINK** before you speak—be **T**rue, **H**elpful, **I**nspiring, **N**ecessary, and **K**ind.

CONNECT WITH YOUR COMMUNITY

"All of us, at some time or other, need help. Whether we're giving or receiving help, each one of us has something valuable to bring to this world. That's one of the things that connects us as neighbors. In our own way, each of us is a giver and a receiver." — Fred Rogers

Connect with something larger than yourself. Volunteer. Help people. We each have gifts and strengths we can share and sharing with others is connecting. Build a community where everyone is using their strengths to help others.

For example, my son Lincoln created something called the "Good Luck Bear"—one of those huge Teddy bears he could actually crawl into, once we cut it open and took out some of the stuffing. We also had to cut out viewing holes for his eyes, as well as make a big hole in the mouth for him to breathe through.

The Good Luck Bear would walk and dance around the neighborhood while people drove by and honked and waved. Lincoln's way of connecting with our community brought a smile to everyone's face during the pandemic's shelter-in-place phase. He has no idea how many lives he touched with his actions.

CONNECT WITH NATURE

"There's no Wi-Fi in the forest, but you will find a better connection." - Unknown

There's nothing like seeing a one-of-a-kind sunset, noticing the glow of a full moon, or hearing ocean waves crash on the shore. Whenever I take the time to notice nature, I am in awe of its beauty. I also realize there's so much more to this world than just me. I feel connected to something much larger than myself.

Take a nature walk. When you see something interesting—like an oddly shaped tree—focus on it. Study its colors, the texture of its leaves, the size of its roots. Do you hear birds chirping on its branches or the wind rustling through its leaves? Some trees—such as eucalyptus, cedar, and pine—have distinct scents. Can you smell the tree from where you're standing?

Now, did you notice you were so focused on the tree that you didn't have any distracting thoughts? This is a form of mindful meditation—the ability to quiet your mind and focus on something besides your thoughts. It can be as simple as staring out of your window and noticing every little thing—birds, squirrels, cars driving by, people jogging, the sun or rain, the clouds. In fact, set a timer for three minutes and make note of how many things you notice within that time span. Make a game of it.

CONNECT WITH ANIMALS

"What you do makes a difference, and you have to decide what kind of difference you want to make." – Jane Goodall

Studies have shown that caring for pets can reduce stress, anxiety, and depression. When you see a cute animal, you instantly feel happy, right? When I am playing with puppies, I always feel calm.

The responsibility of taking care of a pet can help children grow up more secure and active. For example, pets require a regular feeding and exercise schedule. Furthermore, dogs love exercise, and daily exercise is a great way to keep your mind and body healthy.

If you don't have a pet, there are some creative ways to connect with animals, such as volunteering at an animal shelter, visiting a dog park, reading about your favorite animals online, and helping with your friends' pets.

CONNECT WITH THE EARTH

"You may say I'm a dreamer, but I'm not the only one. I hope someday you'll join us, and the world will live as one." — John Lennon

Take some time to appreciate nature. Take some time to look up fun facts about the Earth that interest you. You can also...

CELEBRATE TREES. The next time you go outside, notice the different trees in your neighborhood. Are there big ones and small ones? Do they all have leaves? Does one provide more shade than another? Did you know that trees give off oxygen and absorb carbon dioxide? They are natural air purifiers.

CONSUME FRUITS AND VEGGIES. You've probably heard the saying, "You are what you eat." When you fill your body with healthy foods from the earth, you are keeping your body healthy. The earth becomes part of you when you eat something that has grown from it. We are all connected!

GROW SOMETHING YOURSELF. Whether it's in the house or outside, try growing a plant, a flower, some herbs, or vegetables. We grow tomatoes, sage, rosemary, and garlic in our backyard. The kids take turns watering them every morning. It's fun to watch something grow over time, and also use it when we are cooking.

CONNECT WITH TECHNOLOGY

"We're here to put a dent in the Universe.
Otherwise, why else even be here?" — Steve Jobs

Technology makes it easy to stay connected to others—which was especially handy during the pandemic. Everyone used it to stay connected to families, friends, work, and school.

Technology also helps us connect to the outside world. We literally have the world at our fingertips with the ability to search for knowledge online. I use the Internet to look for things I want to learn more about, or for new skills I want to try, and for research when writing books.

However, while we are connected in more ways than ever before, we are also oddly *disconnected*. Instead of talking in person or on the phone, we communicate by texting. While this can be a useful timesaving tool, it is possible to overuse it.

As with everything else, we must find a balance and learn to use technology wisely. We can stay connected using technology, but we should be mindful about not letting it take over. Take some time every day to disconnect from your screens. Call a friend, go for a walk, or work on being creative. The "Do Not Disturb" feature on many smartphones is a helpful tool. Use this feature during mealtimes and break times.

CONNECT WITH MINDFULNESS

"Almost everything will work again if you unplug it for a few minutes—including you."
– Anne Lamott

We've been hearing the word "mindful" a lot, but what does it mean? To be mindful means being aware of your thoughts and emotions. Being mindful is also having an awareness of the present moment and paying attention to it.

You can practice mindfulness in as little as one minute every day. Stop what you're doing. Take a deep breath. Relax your shoulders. Notice your surroundings. This exercise should help you become aware of the many health benefits to mindfulness—such as reducing stress and improving sleep.

Mindfulness exercises can also get help us get better at understanding our thoughts, feelings, and body sensations. As a result, instead of being overwhelmed by situations, we're better able to manage them. Eventually, try to increase your mindfulness time to two minutes, then five minutes, then ten minutes. Some people even do this exercise for 30 minutes or more a day! It is time well spent, as being mindful can boost attention and concentration, and improve relationships.

CONNECT WITH CREATIVITY

"Music in the soul can be heard by the Universe." – Lao Tzu

Creativity evokes joy within your body. Your creativity comes from your passion. What are you passionate about? You can have many passions. Choose one and start learning about it.

For example, I love the way cars look, so I sometimes try to design cars by looking at pictures online. I also watch movies about racing. I love learning new things about my passion for cars.

I'm also passionate about music. I listen to music every day—whether it's in the car or when I'm in the kitchen.

My daughter London and I love to bake together. She's very adventurous in the kitchen—baking things like beignets, mochi cakes, and lemon bars from scratch—and whenever we bake, we always have music on. We've created a playlist of our favorite songs, and we're always singing and dancing in the kitchen.

Whether you are baking, painting, singing, dancing, or writing, you are connecting with the Universe. As you bring something to life with your creativity, you are also bringing yourself to life.

CONNECT WITH HEALING

"Healing yourself is connected with healing others." - Yoko Ono

Share your experiences—both good and bad—with people you trust. Your experiences may help someone who is going through the same thing, but perhaps hasn't realized it yet. Sharing experiences is how we can help heal each other, heal the earth, and heal ourselves.

For example, perhaps you're scared about something and afraid to talk about it. Talking about your fear with parents, sibling, family members, or friends can help you feel calm and perhaps offer some good advice for not being scared—or at least help you to better deal with your fear. They may even have the same fears as you and your conversation may end up helping both of you!

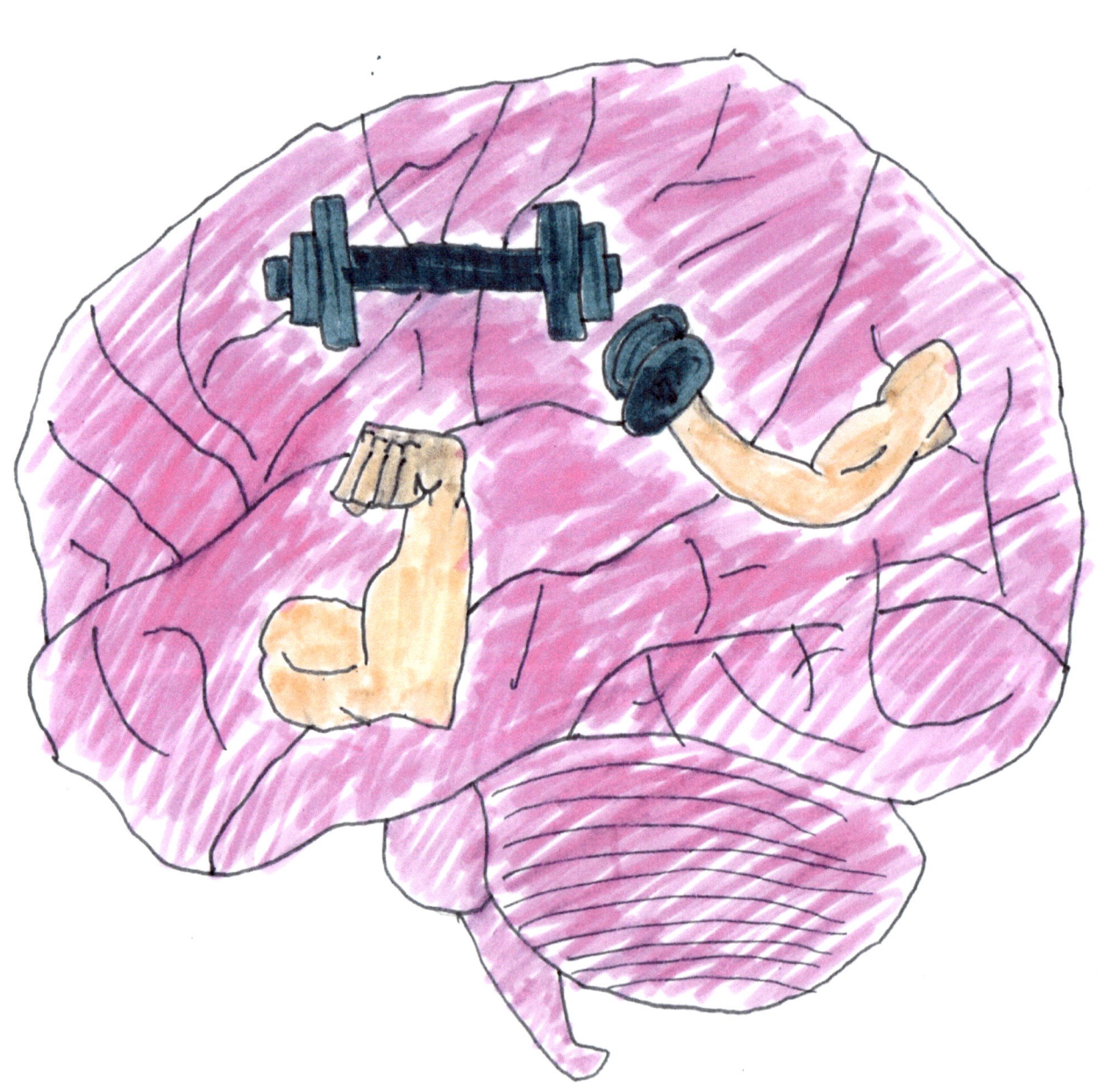

CONNECT WITH MENTAL FITNESS

"Challenge your mind, change your state of being." — Salpi Dunlap

Physical fitness means that we achieve good health and strength through physical exercise. But how do we keep our minds in shape? It's just as important—if not more so—to stay mentally fit.

In times of high stress—such as dealing with the global pandemic—meditation came in really handy for me. My kids and I travel a lot, but we were stuck at home for most of 2020, so we had to find ways to cope. It was tough to quiet my monkey mind, because it wanted to jump around all over the place!

It was hard for me to focus and stay calm, so I started practicing meditation with my kids. We also went for daily walks together, because it became very important for all of us to spend time outside.

Stay mentally healthy with meditation—or other ways to quiet your monkey mind—and by focusing on your breath and spending time in nature. These tools, and others found in the Stay True series, will help exercise the stillness within our minds.

CONNECT WITH THE PRESENT

*"Do not dwell in the past, do not dream of the future.
Concentrate the mind on the present moment." - Buddha*

We spend a lot of time wishing we could change the past or control the future, but the truth is that we can't. A far healthier thing to do is to connect with the present. Here are some ways you can do this...

CREATE AN ATTITUDE OF GRATITUDE. At the beginning and end of each day, list three things you are grateful for. Let these six things be different every day. Try to think of them and focus on them throughout your day.

DON'T COMPARE YOURSELF TO OTHERS. We are all unique individuals, and we are all special in our own ways.

ACCEPT AND CHERISH COMPLIMENTS. Compliments are little gifts we receive from other people. Say "thank you," and allow yourself to receive the compliment.

SURROUND YOURSELF WITH GOODNESS. Spend time on things you love to do and with people who make your heart smile.

STAY ACTIVE. Exercise is important for the mind and body. Get active for at least 30 minutes a day.

SPREAD THE LOVE. Be kind! It's amazing how good we feel when we make someone else feel good.

THOUGHTFUL QUESTIONS

Here is a list of questions for kids and adults to engage in thoughtful conversations. These questions will have different answers every time you ask them. Discuss one or two different questions each night.

- What is one way you are influenced by your peers?
- How do you influence your peers?
- Whose social media profile do you visit most often? Why?
- If you could travel back in time to give yourself advice, what would you tell yourself?
- What makes you feel really stressed? What can you do about it?
- What makes you feel really happy? Why?
- We have the power to create change just by sharing our stories. What's your story? How do you share it with others?
- If you could own only four possessions for the rest of your life, what would they be?
- What did you create today?
- What did you fail at today?
- What would you say to your past self if they were in front of you today?
- What is your favorite quote?
- What is a moment in your life that has changed you?
- What is the best advice someone has given you?
- Who are you grateful for and why?
- How do you inspire others?

ABOUT THE AUTHOR

Salpi is the mother of three beautiful children. She started on her spiritual journey years ago, but didn't realize it until 2016. Since then, she has started practicing being grateful and present. Gratitude and living in the moment have really changed her perspective on happiness. Her quality of life has greatly improved, and all she really did was change the way she looks at things.

Her intent is to share this message with people of all ages. It's never too early or too late to start staying true.

Her three children—Logan, London, and Lincoln—are the illustrators of this book. Salpi wrote the words, and then asked them to draw whatever came to mind to portray the words on the page. The result was pure magic.

www.ingramcontent.com/pod-product-compliance
Lightning Source LLC
Chambersburg PA
CBHW061403090426
42743CB00003B/126